All About Dinosaurs

Tyrannosaurus Rex

Daniel Nunn

Heinemann
LIBRARY

Chicago, Illinois

Edited by Daniel Nunn and James Benefield
Designed by Tim Bond
Picture research by Tracy Cummins
Production by Helen McCreath
Originated by Capstone Global Library Ltd
Printed and bound in China by Leo Paper Group

18 17 16 15 14
10 9 8 7 6 5 4 3 2 1

Library of Congress Cataloging-in-Publication Data
Nunn, Daniel, author.
  Tyrannosaurus rex / Daniel Nunn.
     pages cm.—(All about dinosaurs)
  Summary: "This book takes a very simple look at the
Tyrannosaurus rex dinosaur, examining what it looked
like, what it ate, how it behaved, and its special skills
and features such as its enormous teeth and powerful
jaws. The book also discusses how we know about
Tyrannosaurus rex today, showing where fossils are
found and how scientists put them together."—Provided
by publisher.
  Includes bibliographical references and index.
  ISBN 978-1-4846-0207-2 (hb)—ISBN 978-1-4846-0214-
0 (pb) 1. Tyrannosaurus rex—Juvenile literature. 2.
Dinosaurs—Juvenile literature. I. Title.

QE862.S3N865 2015
567.912'9—dc23   2013040468

Acknowledgments
We would like to thank the following for permission to
reproduce photographs: Getty Images pp. 9 (ROGER
HARRIS), 17 (Jay P. Morgan), 18, 23 (Richard Nowitz);
Science Source pp. 4 (José Antonio Peñas), 20 (Harold
Brodrick); Shutterstock pp. 5a, 13 (DM7), 5b (Maria
Dryfhout), 5c (Karen Givens), 5d, 23 (Piotr Gatlik), 7
bottom (Svinkin), 7 top (Sofia Santos), 8 (Elenarts), 10, 12
(TsuneoMP), 11, 14 (Bob Orsillo), 16 (MaksiMages), 19
(hans engbers); Superstock pp. 6 (NHPA), 15 (Stocktrek
Images), 21 (Tips Images).

Cover photograph of Tyrannosaurus rex, reproduced
with permission of Getty Images (ROGER HARRIS/SPL).

Back cover photograph of Tyrannosaurus rex
reproduced with permission of Shutterstock (Elenarts).

We would like to thank Dee Reid and Nancy Harris for
their invaluable help in the preparation of this book.

Every effort has been made to contact copyright holders
of material reproduced in this book. Any omissions will
be rectified in subsequent printings if notice is given to
the publisher.

006946LEOF14

Contents

Meet Tyrannosaurus Rex

Tyrannosaurus rex was a dinosaur.
Dinosaurs lived long ago.

dinosaur

snake

crocodile

lizard

Dinosaurs were reptiles.
Snakes, crocodiles, and lizards
are reptiles that live today.

What Was Tyrannosaurus Rex Like?

Tyrannosaurus rex was a very big dinosaur.

Tyrannosaurus rex was longer than a bus!

Tyrannosaurus rex had strong
back legs.

Tyrannosaurus rex was fast.

tail

Tyrannosaurus rex had a long tail.

Tyrannosaurus rex's tail stopped it from falling over.

arms

Tyrannosaurus rex had short arms.

teeth

Tyrannosaurus rex had very sharp teeth.

Tyrannosaurus rex had a strong bite.

Tyrannosaurus rex ate other dinosaurs.

Where Is Tyrannosaurus Rex Now?

Tyrannosaurus rex are extinct. There are no Tyrannosaurs rex alive now.

All the dinosaurs died long ago.

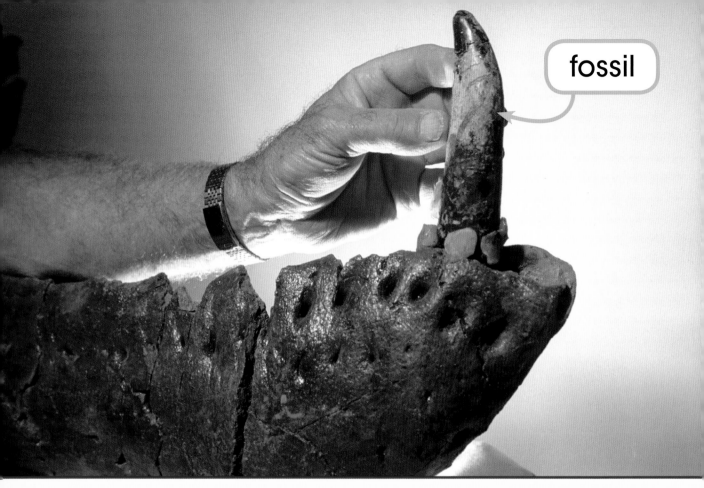

fossil

We learn about Tyrannosaurus rex from fossils.

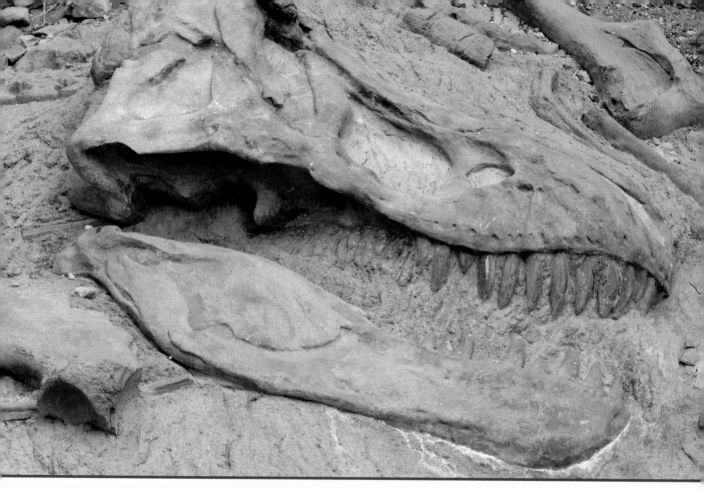

Fossils are animal bones that have turned to rock.

People find fossils in the ground.

Fossils show us what Tyrannosaurus rex looked like.

Where in the World?

Mongolia

North America

Tyrannosaurus rex fossils have been found in North America and Mongolia.

Picture Glossary

 **fossil** animal bones or parts of a plant that have turned into rock

 **reptile** cold-blooded animal. A lizard is a reptile.

How to Say It

Tyrannosaurus rex: say

"tie-ran-uh-sawr-us rex"

Index

Notes for Parents and Teachers

Before reading

Ask the children to name some dinosaurs. Ask them if dinosaurs are around today. Talk about how some dinosaurs ate plants and others ate other dinosaurs. Can they think of ways these dinosaurs might have been different? Have they heard of Tyrannosaurus rex? Find out if they already know anything about this dinosaur.

After reading

- Make Tyrannosaurus rex sock puppets. Give each child a sock and ask the children to stick eyes on each side of the head and lots of sharp teeth in the mouth. They can add small arms at the front. Get the children to ask their puppet questions about what it was like to be a Tyrannosaurus rex.
- Make Tyrannosaurus rex teeth out of clay. They should be at least as long as a child's hand! Make sure they are sharp and then put the dry "fossils" in your own museum.